BEARS

Published by Creative Education, Inc., 123 South Broad Street, Mankato, Minnesota 56001

Printed by permission of Wildlife Education, Ltd.

ISBN 0-88682-221-1

BEARS

Created and Written by
John Bonnett Wexo

Zoological Consultant
Charles R. Schroeder, D.V.M.
Director Emeritus
San Diego Zoo &
San Diego Wild Animal Park

Scientific Consultants
John Craighead, Ph. D.
Director
Wildlife Wildlands Institute

John Mitchell, Ph. D.
Assistant Director
Wildlife Wildlands Institute

Creative Education

Art Credits

Pages Six and Seven: Lisa French; **Page Eight:** Lisa French; **Lower Left,** Walter Stuart; **Page Nine:** Lisa French; **Upper Right,** Walter Stuart; **Page Ten:** Lisa French; **Page Eleven:** Lisa French; **Middle Right,** Walter Stuart; **Page Twelve:** Lisa French; **Page Thirteen:** Lisa French; **Middle Right,** Walter Stuart; **Page Sixteen:** Lisa French; **Page Seventeen:** Lisa French; **Line Art,** Walter Stuart; **Page Eighteen:** Lisa French; **Page Nineteen:** Lisa French; **Upper Right,** Walter Stuart; **Pages Twenty and Twenty-One:** Walter Stuart; **Teddy Bear Sketch** by Clifton Berryman: Courtesy of Library of Congress; **All Maps** by Andy Lucas.

Photographic Credits

Front Cover: © 1986 EPI Nancy Adams *(Tom Stack & Associates);* **Page Eleven:** R.F. Head *(Animals Animals);* **Page Thirteen:** Martin W. Grosnick *(Ardea London);* **Pages Fourteen and Fifteen:** Zig Leszczynski *(Animals Animals);* **Pages Sixteen and Seventeen:** Joe Rychetnik *(Photo Researchers);* **Page Eighteen: Upper Left,** Courtesy of Brookfield Zoo; **Upper Right,** Charles VanValkenburgh/Wildlife Education, Ltd.; **Page Nineteen: Upper Left,** Courtesy of Los Angeles Zoo; **Center Right,** Tom McHugh *(Photo Researchers);* **Page Twenty: Lower Left,** Charles VanValkenburgh/Wildlife Education, Ltd.; **Upper Right,** Willard Luce *(Animals Animals);* **Page Twenty-One:** H. Armstrong Roberts; **Pages Twenty-Two and Twenty-Three:** Masahiri Iijima *(Ardea London).*

Our Thanks To: Mrs. Diane Chrysler *(and "Edward");* William Cunningham *(Wilderness Society Montana);* Gary Brown and the staff of the Yellowstone Park Bear Project; Clifford Martinka *(Glacier National Park);* Clyde Lockwood *(Glacier National History Association);* Dr. David Fagan; Lynnette Wexo.

Special Thanks To: Michaele Robinson, Librarian of the Zoological Society of San Diego, and her staff.

Creative Education would like to thank Wildlife Education, Ltd., for granting them the rights to print and distribute this hardbound edition.

Contents

SLOTH BEAR
Melursus ursinus

Bears have been great favorites in zoos for hundreds of years, and it's not hard to see why this is so. Their great strength is impressive to many people, and the sheer size of some bears is enough to gain instant respect. What's more, a bear can look remarkably like a giant person when it stands up on its hind feet...and this is certainly intriguing.

Male bears are called boars, and females are called sows. Young bears, of course, are called cubs. Sows are usually smaller than boars—and as a rule, they stay away from the larger males. Only during the mating season do sows and boars spend any time together.

The largest of the bears are the biggest meat-

ALASKA BROWN BEAR
Ursus arctos

POLAR BEAR
Ursus maritimus

MALAYAN SUN BEAR
Helarctos malayanus

SPECTACLED BEAR
Tremarctos ornatus

AMERICAN BLACK BEAR
Ursus americanus

eating land animals on earth, by a wide margin. A large tiger may weigh about 770 pounds (349 kilograms), but a big bear can weigh *almost three times as much.*

For many years, the Kodiak brown bear was called the giant of the bears, weighing up to 1,600 pounds (726 kilograms) and standing as much as 11 feet tall (3.35 meters). But it now appears that polar bears can be even larger. A polar bear shot in 1962 was over 11 feet tall (3.39 meters) and weighed an incredible *2,210 pounds* (1,002 kilograms). The smallest of the bears is the sun bear of Malaya, which is only 4 feet tall (1.2 meters) and weighs less than 100 pounds (45 kilograms).

ASIATIC BLACK BEAR
Selenarctos thibetanus

GRIZZLY BEAR
AND NURSING CUBS
Ursus arctos

Bears have short but powerful legs. A huge brown bear can run at a speed of 35 miles (56 kilometers) per hour for short distances—fast enough to catch a running horse.

The body of a bear may look lumpy and clumsy, but these animals are among the strongest and fastest on earth. It is strange that such powerful creatures are so peaceful by nature. Usually, they will only fight when they have to. They rarely attack large animals.

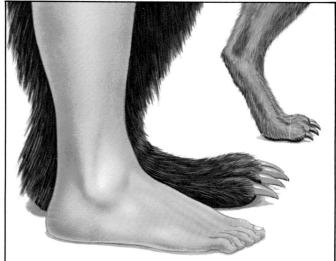

Like humans, bears put their feet down flat on the ground when they walk. Scientists call this flat-footed walk a plantigrade (PLANT-uh-grade) walk. Most other large animals (including dogs, horses, and even elephants) walk on their toes. The flat-footed stance of bears makes it easy for them to stand up straight as humans do . . . although they rarely walk when standing up.

The claws on the front feet of bears are longer than the claws on the back feet. Some large bears have claws almost 5 inches (13 centimeters) long. But as dangerous as these weapons can be in a fight, bears use them most of the time for digging up food or catching fish.

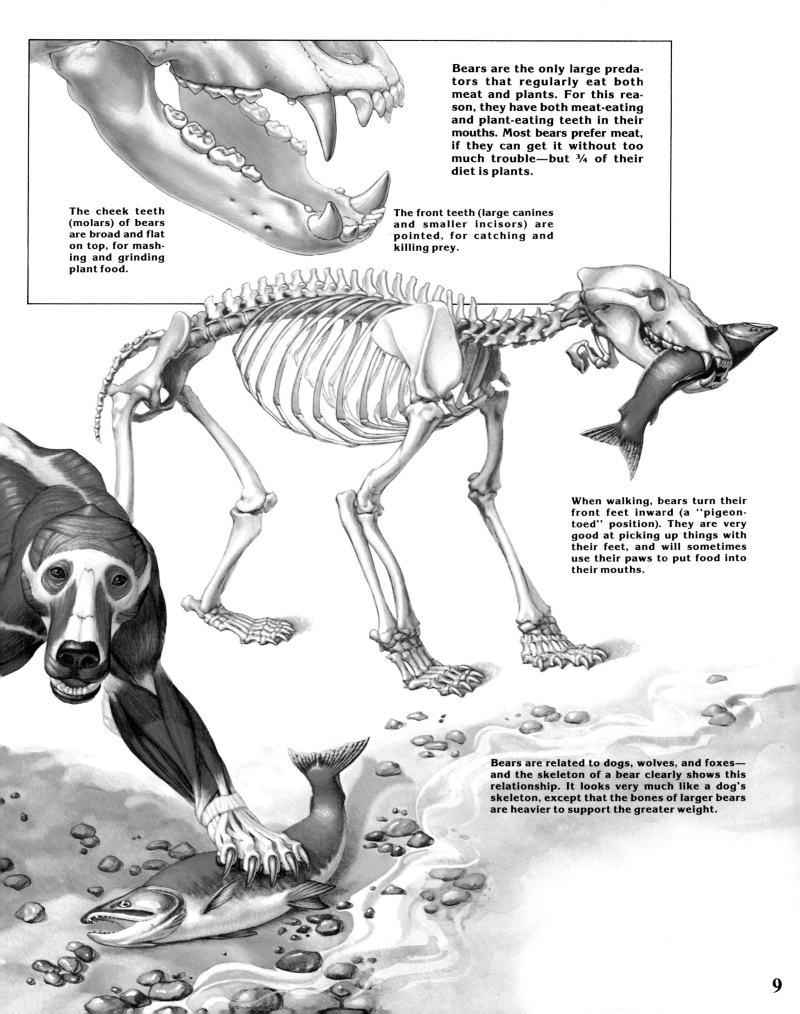

Bears are the only large predators that regularly eat both meat and plants. For this reason, they have both meat-eating and plant-eating teeth in their mouths. Most bears prefer meat, if they can get it without too much trouble—but ¾ of their diet is plants.

The cheek teeth (molars) of bears are broad and flat on top, for mashing and grinding plant food.

The front teeth (large canines and smaller incisors) are pointed, for catching and killing prey.

When walking, bears turn their front feet inward (a "pigeon-toed" position). They are very good at picking up things with their feet, and will sometimes use their paws to put food into their mouths.

Bears are related to dogs, wolves, and foxes—and the skeleton of a bear clearly shows this relationship. It looks very much like a dog's skeleton, except that the bones of larger bears are heavier to support the greater weight.

9

Black bears are small bears, compared to their cousins the brown and polar bears. They usually weigh no more than 300 pounds (136 kilograms), and are less than 5½ feet long (1.7 meters). They have long, straight noses and the largest ears of any bears.

Trees are a black bear's best friends. Whenever they are in danger, black bears climb trees. They have rather short claws that are ideal for scrambling up a tree trunk. It is not surprising that black bears stay as close to trees as they can. They rarely leave the forest.

Like other bears that live in colder parts of the world, black bears spend the winter in a den. In September, they find a cave or other existing hole in the ground. They drag leaves and tree branches into the hole to make a bed. And about a month later, when the heavy snows come, they crawl into their den and go to sleep. They may stay asleep without eating or drinking for as long as 6 months. This "deep sleep" is often called hibernation (HI-BUR-NAY-SHUN).

During the coldest part of the winter, black bear babies are born in the den. Usually, two babies are born at one time, but there can be from one to four cubs in a litter. The babies are very small, often weighing less than ½ pound (226 grams) at birth.

Baby black bears are blind and covered with very fine hair when they are born. They look almost naked. While winter storms rage outside the den, their mother's body heat keeps them warm, and they grow very rapidly. By the time they leave the den in spring, they are strong and playful. The first day outside, they may even start climbing trees!

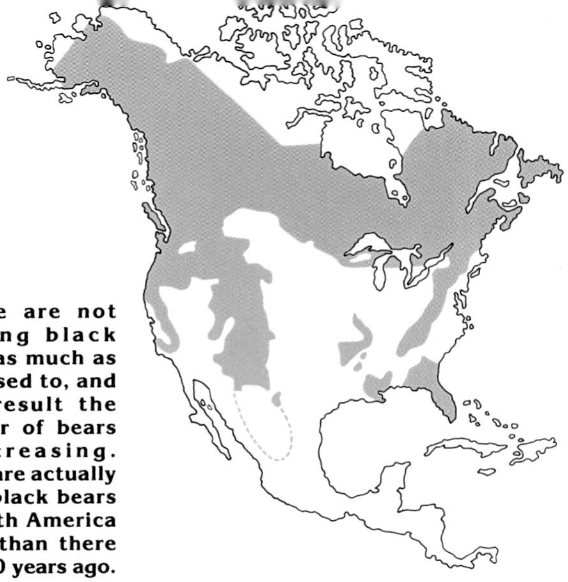

People are not hunting black bears as much as they used to, and as a result the number of bears is increasing. There are actually more black bears in North America today than there were 50 years ago.

KERMODE'S BEAR

BLUE (OR GLACIER) BEAR

CINNAMON BEAR

STANDARD BLACK BEAR

Black bears aren't always black. Varieties of the black bear, found in different parts of North America, can have very different colors. There's even a black bear that is white!

The dens of different kinds of bears are different. Most black bears use a cave or a hole that has been opened by a falling tree. Brown bears nearly always dig a hole for themselves. Polar bears usually hollow out a snowbank, and the warmth of their breath often creates a vent in the roof to let in fresh air.

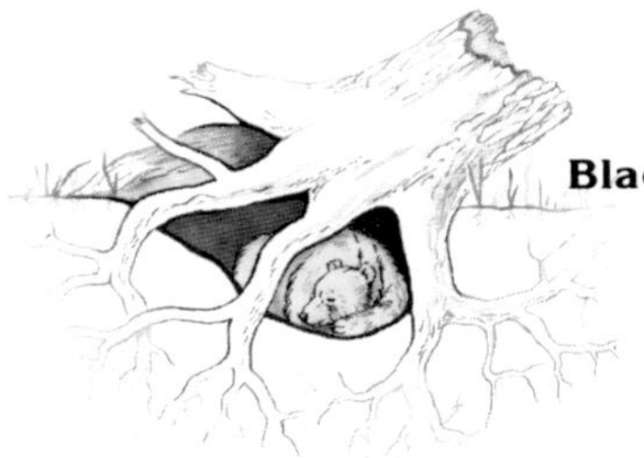

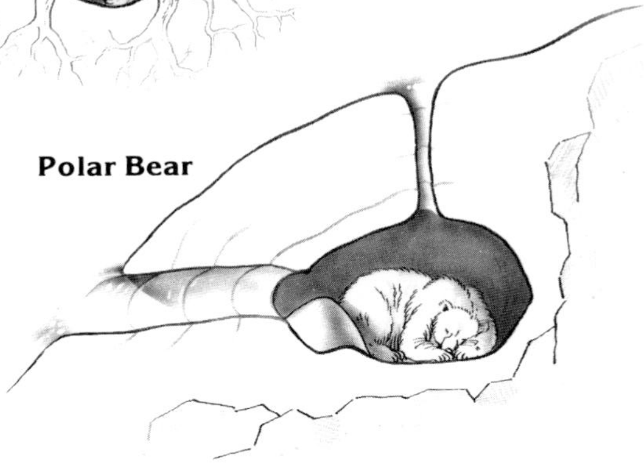

Black Bear

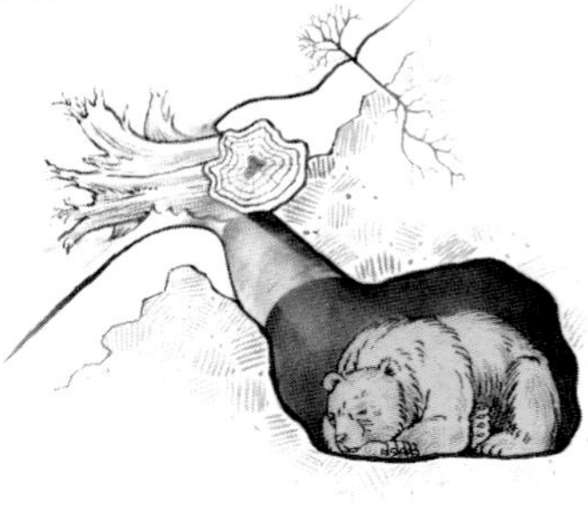

Polar Bear

Brown Bear

Asiatic black bears are smaller than North American black bears. And longer hair on their necks and chests makes them look very different. Some people call them "moon bears," because they have white moon-shaped crescent markings on their chests. They live in mountain forests of southern Asia.

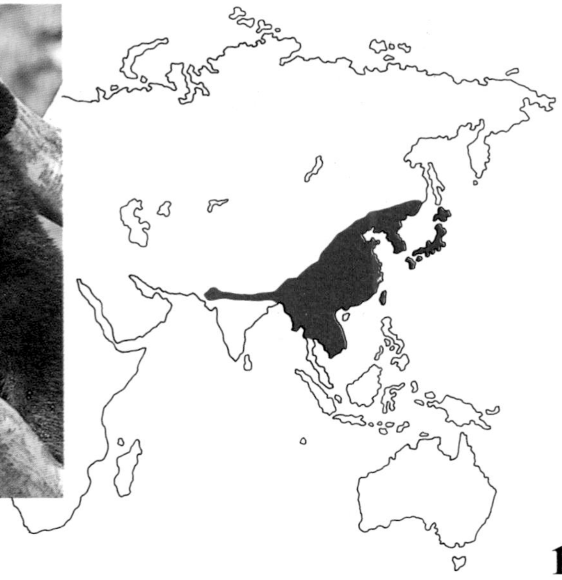

Brown bears are probably descended from the black bear family, but they do not stay in the forest as much as black bears do. Instead, they seem to prefer open meadows, river valleys, and even treeless plains. They are less timid than black bears, and more likely to fight if they feel they are being threatened.

There are many different sizes of brown bears. In Europe, they are only a little larger than black bears—but some of the brown bears of Asia and Alaska are giants. The famous Grizzly bear, which is actually a middle-sized brown bear, is found only in North America.

All brown bears have a large hump of muscle and fat over the shoulders. They have small ears and long, thick fur. As with all bears, the females are smaller than the males. And like most other bears, they live alone most of the time (with the exception of females with young cubs).

At the first sign of danger, brown bear mothers generally chase their cubs up a tree. While they are young, brown bears are light enough to climb trees, but when they grow larger they become too heavy to do it anymore.

A newly born Kodiak brown bear can sometimes weigh less than one pound (½ kilogram). As it grows up, however, its weight may increase as much as 1,000 times. If human babies grew this much, adult people would weigh over 6,000 pounds!

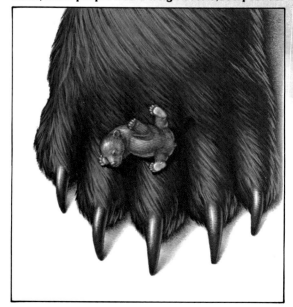

All bear mothers take very good care of their cubs. They are always ready to fight if they think the cubs are in danger. Among the greatest dangers to young bears are adult male bears, who sometimes catch and eat cubs. But even a huge and hungry brown bear male doesn't want to tangle with an angry brown bear mother.

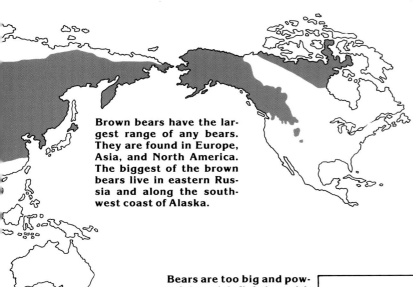

Brown bears have the largest range of any bears. They are found in Europe, Asia, and North America. The biggest of the brown bears live in eastern Russia and along the southwest coast of Alaska.

Brown bears come in many shades of brown. Some, like the one shown here, are almost black. Others can be almost white (and, in fact, some scientists believe that polar bears are descended from light-colored brown bears). Some brown bears have grey (or "grizzled") tips on their hair, and are therefore called Grizzly bears.

Bears are too big and powerful to risk fighting with each other too often. So they have a social system that prevents too much fighting. In a series of short fights, the largest males test each other's strength. The bear that finally wins becomes the "top bear" for a time. The other bears accept a lesser position in bear society, and so fighting is reduced.

Alpha Male ("Top Bear")   Other Males   Sows and Cubs

13

This Malayan Sun Bear cub and its mother make a happy picture. Though adult bears are very strong and aggressive, the mother is quite gentle with her young.

Polar bears are the best hunters of all the bears. They have to be, since they live in areas where plant food is not often available. In general, individual polar bears have larger ranges than other bears, because they must go where the food is. When seals migrate, for instance, polar bears often go along with them.

Since they must sometimes survive very cold temperatures, polar bears have a thick layer of fat under their skin. Unlike other bears, they have good eyesight and they have stiff hair on the bottom of their feet to keep them from slipping on the ice.

The fur of polar bears is not pure white, as many people think. It is actually yellowish. Each hair is hollow to help insulate the bear from the cold.

The light color of its fur helps a polar bear to stay hidden as it stalks its prey. To keep the prey from seeing its dark nose and mouth, a bear sometimes covers them with a paw.

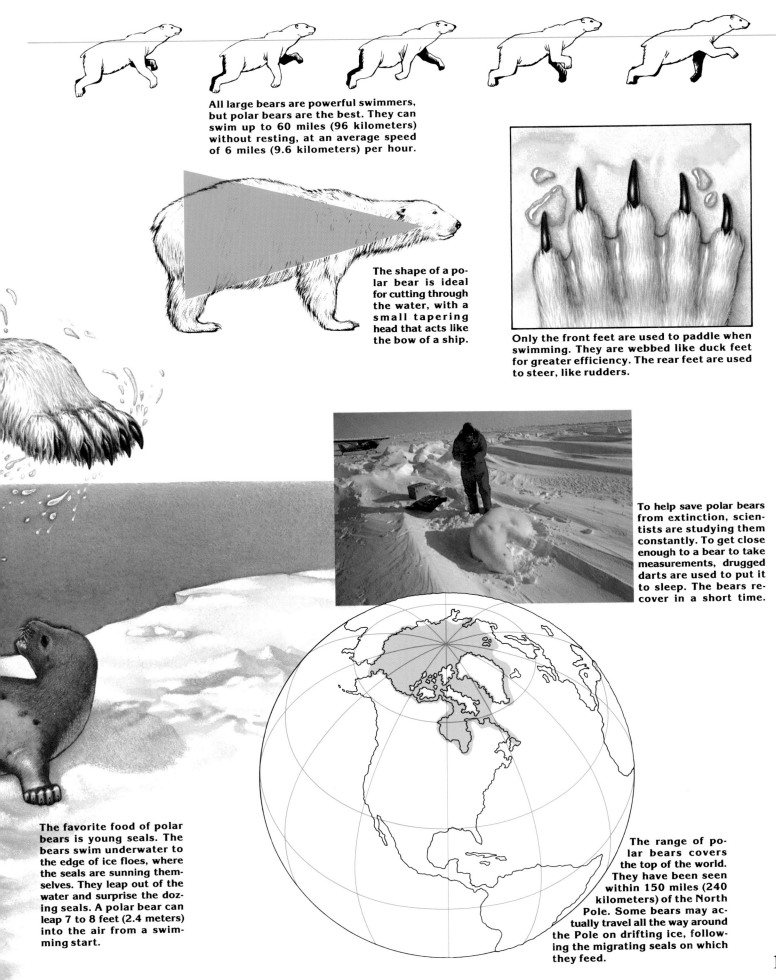

All large bears are powerful swimmers, but polar bears are the best. They can swim up to 60 miles (96 kilometers) without resting, at an average speed of 6 miles (9.6 kilometers) per hour.

The shape of a polar bear is ideal for cutting through the water, with a small tapering head that acts like the bow of a ship.

Only the front feet are used to paddle when swimming. They are webbed like duck feet for greater efficiency. The rear feet are used to steer, like rudders.

To help save polar bears from extinction, scientists are studying them constantly. To get close enough to a bear to take measurements, drugged darts are used to put it to sleep. The bears recover in a short time.

The favorite food of polar bears is young seals. The bears swim underwater to the edge of ice floes, where the seals are sunning themselves. They leap out of the water and surprise the dozing seals. A polar bear can leap 7 to 8 feet (2.4 meters) into the air from a swimming start.

The range of polar bears covers the top of the world. They have been seen within 150 miles (240 kilometers) of the North Pole. Some bears may actually travel all the way around the Pole on drifting ice, following the migrating seals on which they feed.

The three smallest bears look very different from each other, but they really have a lot in common. For example, all three spend a lot of their time up in trees. They do not hibernate like other bears do. And all three live for about the same number of years—up to 20 years.

As far as we know, spectacled bears are the only bears that eat no meat. They live in the high mountains of South America, while the other two types of bears live in lowland forests of Asia.

Spectacled bears get their name from light-colored streaks around their eyes that sometimes look like eyeglasses. The markings on each bear are unique, like fingerprints, and can be used to tell one bear from another.

Spectacled Bear

Sloth Bear

Sun Bear

All bears love honey, but the sun bear loves it most of all. In fact, the common name for this bear in southeast Asia is "honey bear." When it tears into a beehive with its long claws, the bear isn't bothered by bee stings. It just eats the bees along with the honey!

Most bears live alone most of the time, but the sloth (SLOW-th) bear is different. It seems to like the company of other sloth bears. And while male bears usually don't stay with females long enough to see what their cubs look like, the father sloth bear stays around to help raise his offspring. Sloth bears are also the only bears that regularly carry their young from place to place on their backs.

Young sun bears are cute and playful, and this makes them popular pets in Asia. But as they grow up, they become hard to handle and usually have to be given to a zoo. Wild animals in general do not make good pets for this reason.

Spectacled bears are the only bears from South America, and along with sun bears are the only bears found in the Southern Hemisphere. The ranges of all three bears are shrinking.

"Bears" that Aren't Bears

Even though they look like bears in many ways, pandas and koalas are not bears. Most scientists feel that the panda is more closely related to raccoons than bears. And the koala is a marsupial (mar-SOOP-ee-ul) from Australia. (Notice the strange un-bearlike hands and feet of the koala.)

People can't make up their minds

about bears. On the one hand, we see them as dangerous beasts who will kill us if we don't watch out. On the other hand, we see them as animals that are cuddly and furry, and that can walk upright like people. Neither of our attitudes toward bears has been good for the bears.

People who see them as monsters feel that they should hunt bears, while people who see them as furry people feel that bears should be petted and coddled. Either way, we are pushing the bears to be *what we want them to be*, instead of what they really are.

People who think bears are cute insist on feeding them or teasing them when they visit a national park. When some of these people get hurt, they usually blame it on the bears.

Hundreds of years ago, before lions were known in Europe, the bear was called the "King of Beasts." The picture of a bear on a flag or a coat of arms was meant to indicate power. Many towns in Europe named themselves after bears and proudly took the bear as their symbol. This is the coat of arms of the city of Bern (which means "bear") in Switzerland.

Stone-age hunters worshipped and hunted bears at the same time. To overcome the great power of the bear, they sang and danced and prayed that the bear would forgive them for killing it.

In 1902, the 26th President of the United States refused to shoot a black bear while out hunting. So popular was Theodore Roosevelt that toy bears were created to celebrate the event. And so was born the Teddy (Roosevelt) Bear. Strange to say, almost all teddy bears are brown instead of black.

In Asia, black bear cubs are often taken from their mothers at an early age to be trained as dancing bears. The ability of bears to stand up on their hind feet makes it possible for them to shuffle around in a way that looks something like a human dance.

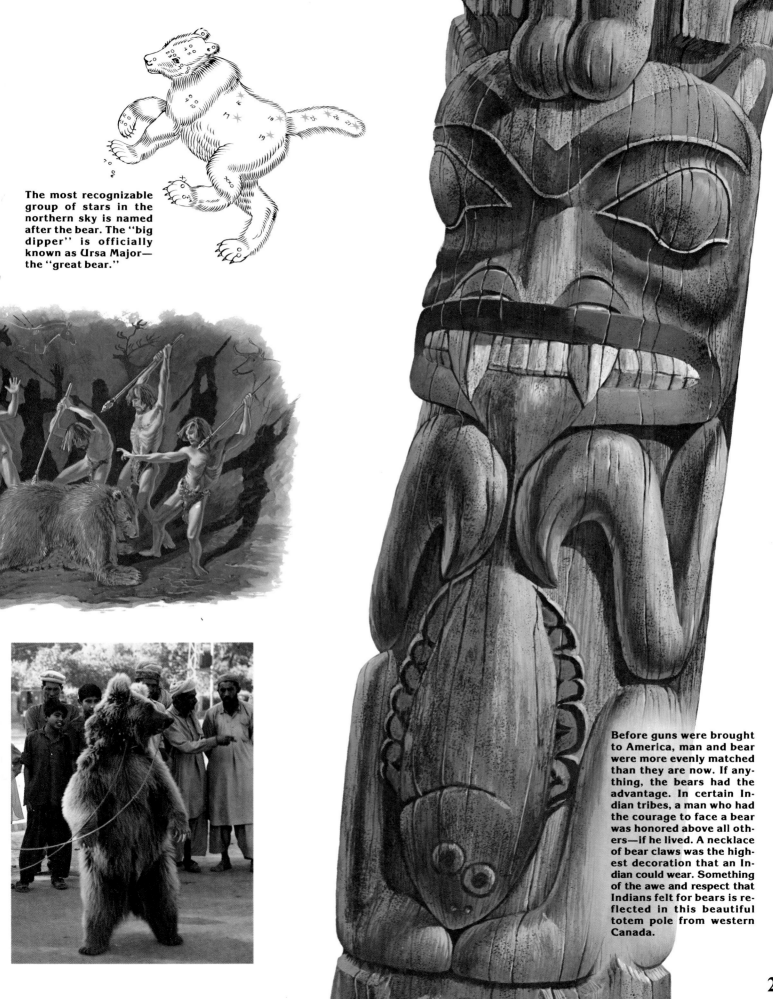

The most recognizable group of stars in the northern sky is named after the bear. The "big dipper" is officially known as Ursa Major—the "great bear."

Before guns were brought to America, man and bear were more evenly matched than they are now. If anything, the bears had the advantage. In certain Indian tribes, a man who had the courage to face a bear was honored above all others—if he lived. A necklace of bear claws was the highest decoration that an Indian could wear. Something of the awe and respect that Indians felt for bears is reflected in this beautiful totem pole from western Canada.

The future of bears is up to us. Because it is the human desire for more land and resources that is the main threat to the survival of bears throughout the world.

Until recently, most bears had no competition for living space and food. There were no animals big enough and fierce enough to keep a big bear from going where it wanted to go and eating what it wanted to eat. But people, with guns and technology, have changed all that.

As the number of people on earth has grown, the human need for living space, food, energy, and resources has grown along with it. More and more land has been taken from the wild and turned into farms and cities. Vast forests have been cut down. Modern industries have polluted the land, the air, and the water in many places.

Most animals have suffered from this destruction of wild land. But big meat-eating animals—like bears—have suffered the most. A big bear must have a large area in which to find its food, because it needs a very large amount of food to stay alive. And since bears eat a wide variety of different kinds of food, they are very dependent on the general well-being of all animals and plants in the region they occupy.

For these reasons, it really doesn't take much to make a region unfit for bears. An oil-drilling rig or a highway may bring so many people into an area that its ecological balance is disrupted. In the arctic, an oil spill from a tanker may kill enough seals to lead to the starvation of the polar bears that usually feed on the seals.

In the past, bears have coped with the problem of man by living in wild places where people could not comfortably live. But now, with improved technology and an increasing need for energy and other resources, man is rapidly moving into these last remote places. There are literally no longer any places where bears can be safe from people.

So the issue is clear: if we want to have bears in this world, *it is up to us to leave room for bears*. We must try to protect the wilderness and continue to set aside areas for bears where people are only visitors—places that bears can call home and where they are still the most powerful animals.

22

ASIATIC BLACK BEAR

Index